Be INSPIRED!

YOUNG IRISH PEOPLE CHANGING THE WORLD

SARAH WEBB

ILLUSTRATED BY

GRAHAM CORCORAN

A portion of the royalties for this book
are being donated to

children's
books
ireland
every child a reader

THE O'BRIEN PRESS
DUBLIN

About the Author

Sarah Webb LOVES books! She is an award-winning children's writer, and her books include *Blazing a Trail: Irish Women who Changed the World* (illustrated by Lauren O'Neill) and *A Sailor Went to Sea, Sea, Sea: Favourite Rhymes from an Irish Childhood* (illustrated by Steve McCarthy), both winners of Irish Book Awards, and *Dare to Dream: Irish People Who Took on the World (and Won!)* illustrated by Graham Corcoran. She runs creative writing clubs for children and teens, reviews children's books for the *Irish Independent*, and programmes children's and family events for book festivals and MoLI (Museum of Literature Ireland). She also works part-time in a children's bookshop, Halfway Up the Stairs, where she is Events Manager.

Sarah is passionate about bringing children and books together and was awarded the Children's Books Ireland Award for Outstanding Contribution to Children's Books in Ireland. www.sarahwebb.ie

About the Illustrator

Graham Corcoran is an illustrator based in Dublin, Ireland. He has previously illustrated the award-nominated children's book *Dare to Dream* written by Sarah Webb, the award-winning *The Story of Croke Park* written by Mícheál Ó Muircheartaigh, both published by The O'Brien Press, and *The Great Irish Politics Book* written by David McCullagh. He has also designed several animated children's series for RTÉ, BBC, Sky and Nick Jr.

Also by Sarah Webb from The O'Brien Press:
Dare to Dream (illustrated by Graham Corcoran)
Blazing a Trail (illustrated by Lauren O'Neill)
Sally Go Round the Stars (illustrated by Steve McCarthy)
A Sailor Went to Sea, Sea, Sea (illustrated by Steve McCarthy)
The One with the Waggly Tail (illustrated by Steve McCarthy)
The Little Bee Charmer of Henrietta Street (illustrated by Rachel Corcoran)
Emma the Penguin (illustrated by Anne O'Hara)

Illustrated by Graham Corcoran from The O'Brien Press:
Dare to Dream (written by Sarah Webb)
The Story of Croke Park (written by Mícheál Ó Muircheartaigh)

ABOUT THIS BOOK

Working on *Be Inspired*, researching and talking to some of the young people within its pages was a great privilege and an experience I will never forget.

From the start, I knew I wanted the book to reflect Ireland now, a different Ireland to the country I grew up in. A new Ireland that strives to support and celebrate children and young people of all colours, genders, heritages and abilities. A country for everyone. We have made a start as a more inclusive country, but we still have a long way to go.

Many of the young people in this book have faced physical or mental challenges and have succeeded regardless. But there are extra challenges life throws at some young people. I had to ask some interviewees how they deal with discrimination including racism. I wish it wasn't a relevant question.

I hope I did all the young people featured in this book justice. I hope I captured their amazing spirit, energy and passion for life. I believe stepping into another person's shoes and seeing the world through their eyes is one of the great gifts that books can give us.

Be Inspired celebrates twenty-eight remarkable young people; I am so grateful to all those who shared their stories with me. It was also a great honour to meet or talk to some of their incredibly supportive and helpful parents.

I came away changed from many of the interviews. For good. Maybe this book will also change a child's life – showing them that they too can achieve their goals.

I hope every young reader will be inspired to follow their own dreams.

Acknowledgements

This book was very much a team effort and a true labour of love. Thank you to my kind, patient and wise editor, Helen Carr. Helen was aided in her editorial role by Princess Okonkwo and Aoife Harrison. Designer Emma Byrne did an amazing job on the design of *Be Inspired*. Graham Corcoran worked incredibly hard to capture the spirit of each young person.

I'd also like to thank all the young people in *Be Inspire*d and many of their parents. I couldn't have done it without your time, support and kindness. Thank you to all those who helped me with the research for this book, including journalists Cristín Leach and Patrick Freyne, Elaine Burke at Silicon Republic, Colin Armstrong at Paralympics Ireland, Lisa Cook at The Lisa Richards Agency, David King and Juelie McLoughlin, Caoimhe McCabe at Pavee Point, Michelle O'Connor at the Federation of Irish Beekeepers' Associations, and RTÉ reporter, Jennie O'Sullivan.

Dedication

This book is dedicated to Elaina Ryan, Jenny Murray, Aoife Murray and all at Children's Books Ireland past and present for their remarkable work bringing together young people and books. And to my own young people, Sam, Amy-Rose and Jago. With love and respect. *Sarah Webb*

This book is dedicated to my wonderful wife, Nicole, and to my always supportive parents, Paul and Claire. *Graham Corcoran*

CONTENTS

THE ARTS, CULTURE, FASHION

CAMPAIGNERS AND ACTIVISTS

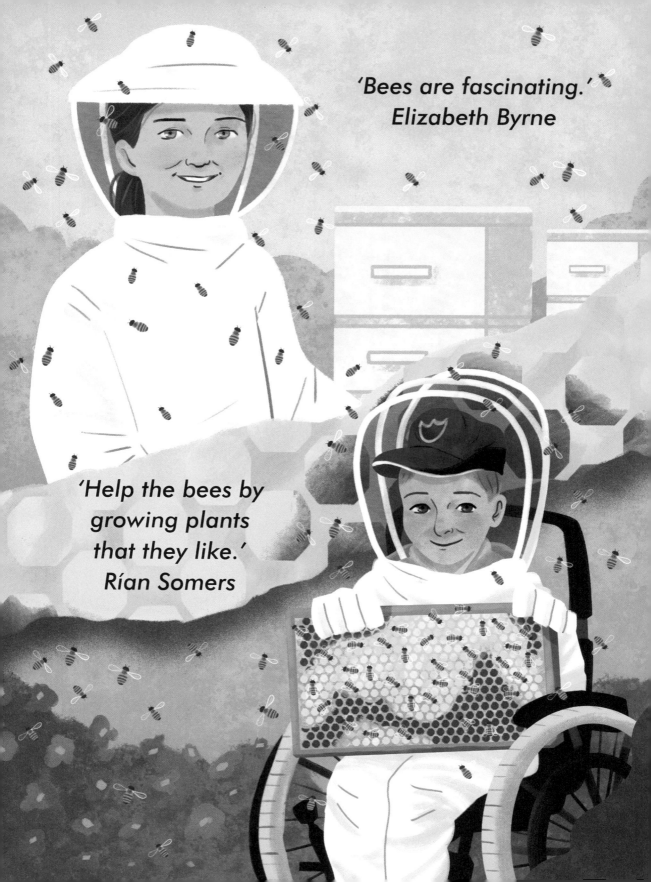

RÍAN SOMERS & ELIZABETH BYRNE

BEEKEEPERS
2014 & 2005

Rían started beekeeping when he was five; he now has two hives of his own, with over 60,000 bees in each! He is Ireland's youngest beekeeper.

His favourite queen bee is called Sofia. 'You can spot her as we put a yellow dot on her tummy,' he says.

Rían was born with spina bifida* and is a wheelchair user, but he doesn't let this stop him. As well as beekeeping, he also loves hurling, drama, fishing, swimming, Beavers and basketball.

When Elizabeth was little, she used to watch insects flying around her garden in Claremorris, Co. Mayo. When she was eight she went to a beekeeping meeting with her dad and was hooked. She was the youngest beekeeper in Ireland to pass the level one beekeeping exam and is now studying for level two and looking after her fifty hives.

'You learn new things about bees nearly every day,' she says. She gets stung sometimes, even when wearing her bee suit, but says, 'You get used to it!'

Elizabeth hopes to study art or photography one day, but she'll always be a beekeeper. 'It's a great hobby to have,' she says. 'I want to learn more and more about bees.'

*Spina bifida is a medical condition that affects the spine. Some people with spina bifida can find it hard to walk.

Elizabeth's Advice:
'Find your local beekeeping association, they will help you set up a hive.'

Elizabeth's honey is called 'Bóthar Dubh Bees' and she sells it when it's in season in September and October.

Rían's honey is called 'Rían's Honey' and the label was designed by his big brother, Calum.

MARGARET & RACHAEL AKANO, JOY NJEKWE

Scientists, Tech Entrepreneurs & Coders

2003, 2004, 2003

Margaret and Rachael Akano and Joy Njekwe entered the Technovation Global Competition for apps in 2019 and failed to be shortlisted. Rather than give up, they entered again in 2020 and won their category, beating 1,500 entries from 62 countries!

How did three girls from Drogheda, Co. Louth achieve this amazing result? Their journey began at a tech summer camp run by their mentor, Evelyn Nomayo (pictured here with the three). They began working on apps together, choosing to create an app for dementia (severe memory loss), which Evelyn's mother suffered from. The Memory Haven app has many features to support people with dementia, including a memory game and a music playlist. They are still working on it and hope it will be on the market in the near future.

Margaret has always wanted to be a doctor and is currently pursuing her goal. Rachael hopes to study multimedia after school. Joy studied Scratch in primary school and found coding great fun. She also 'broke a lot of things as a child' to find out how they worked, and now studies engineering. They all hope that one day girls will be fully represented in the tech industry. 'STEM is for everyone,' Joy says and she's so right!

Rachael was STEM Prefect at her school, the first person to hold this role. She also loves music and is a keen singer. 'Music is everything to me,' she says. 'I can't imagine a world without music.'

After winning Technovation, Margaret, Rachael and Joy were interviewed by national and international media including RTÉ and the BBC. 'It was nice to be able to show young people that they can make a difference.'

Advice for young people who would like to get involved in STEM:
Try everything. If you have an interest in something, find out information and teach yourself. And most importantly: just go for it and don't give up!

'Science is in everything!'
Margaret Akano

'I believe a child-like, playful mindset is exactly what we need to solve some of the problems in the world.'

FIONN FERREIRA

INVENTOR, ENTREPRENEUR & ENVIRONMENTAL ACTIVIST

2000

Fionn Ferreira is from a small village in West Cork and became internationally famous in the science world after winning the 2019 Google Science Fair. He invented a method of removing microplastics* from water using magnetic ferrofluid*. We consume a credit card-sized amount of plastic every week through our water and food, which could have terrible effects on our health in the future.

The idea for Fionn's invention came to him when he spotted an oil spill on a beach rock that had attracted plastic particles; his brain went into overdrive. Ferrofluid, he thought – that could take plastics out of the sea! He began building his own science equipment and the rest is history.

Fionn can't remember a time when he wasn't interested in science and nature. At age seven he started to find animals tangled up in plastic on his local beach. 'Nature was being destroyed by people and no one was doing anything about it.' He wanted to do something to help.

His invention has taken him all over the world, speaking at conferences for organisations like National Geographic and the Smithsonian Museum. Engineers in Ohio, USA are now working on ways to use Fionn's invention, with funding from actor Robert Downey Junior's Footprint Coalition.

Fionn is currently working on several TV shows and his first children's book, which he hopes will inspire young people to take action and protect our amazing planet.

*Microplastics: Tiny plastic particles less than 2mm in diameter (the size of a pencil point).
*Magnetic ferrofluid: A liquid that is attracted to a magnet.

Fionn once blew the electricity in the whole of his village when one of his experiments went wrong. He also took apart his family's washing machine to find microplastics and it's never been the same since!

A minor planet was named after Fionn when he won an award at the International Science and Engineering Fair in 2018. This is very apt as he loves the stars and worked in the Schull Planetarium as a teenager.

Fionn's Advice for Young Inventors:
Inventing is not always about the outcome, it's about the process. 'There is no discovery without failure,' he says. Never be afraid of being at the cutting edge and have fun testing things out!

BT YOUNG SCIENTISTS

In 1963 two physics researchers from University College Dublin, Rev. Dr Tom Burke and Dr Tony Scott, were in New Mexico, America for their work. They came across the idea of 'Science Fairs' for school students and brought the idea back to Ireland.

The first Young Scientist Exhibition was held in 1965 in the Mansion House in Dublin. Two hundred and thirty students entered, and thousands of people visited the exhibition which was sponsored by Aer Lingus.

The following year it moved to the much larger RDS and it has been there ever since. It has been proudly sponsored by BT for over twenty years. In 2022 over 2,000 projects were submitted, an all-time high. It's now one of the largest events of its kind in Europe.

In the 1960s and early 1970s entries from girls and boys went into different categories and entries from girls entering outnumbered boys. Today similar numbers of girls and boys enter, and they are no longer separated into different categories.

Why don't YOU enter? You never know where it might take you!

In 1998 Cork student Raphael Hurley researched Monopoly to see if owning particular properties could help you win. He confirmed that orange properties were the ones to go for. He found that winning is down to luck, not science at all!

The first ever winner of the Young Scientist Exhibition in 1965 was John Monahan from Newbridge College, Co. Kildare. His project examined the human digestive system.

The first female winner was Mary Finn from the Ursuline Convent, Sligo in 1966. Her project studied the 'four colour problem' in topology (mapping), a complex maths problem.

The youngest winner to date is Emer Jones, from Tralee, Co. Kerry. Her project about emergency sandbag shelters won the top prize in 2008 when she was thirteen. She got the idea from news reports about natural disasters. 'I wanted to do a project that could do some good,' she said. She went on to study science at Cambridge University.

'Start now! Don't let your age hold you back.'

JORDAN CASEY

CODER & TECH ENTREPRENEUR
2000

When Jordan Casey was nine years old, he loved Club Penguin, a computer game designed for children. He wanted to design his own website for fellow fans of the game, so he asked his granny to buy him a book about computer programming and he taught himself how to code using HTML. The website was hugely successful and it kickstarted his own company, Casey Games!

'It was hard to be taken seriously sometimes because of my age,' he says. But he kept going.

When he was twelve, he created an iPhone app, Alien vs Humans, which went to number one in the app store in Ireland. He became the youngest iOS developer in Europe and was asked to talk at conferences and events all over the world, from India to Poland.

Although he was shy as a child, he found he was able to talk about his work to large crowds and express himself well. He has spoken at many TEDx events, including in India and Warsaw.

When his teacher in school lost her notebook, it gave him an idea for TeachWare, a cloud-based system for helping teachers manage their students' exam and attendance records.

Other games he has created are Food World and Greenboy. He launched KidsCode in 2016, a multi-player virtual world designed to help teach children to code using online games and puzzles. Recently he designed HUB, a software to help venues like cinemas and theatres run their business.

Always up for a challenge, we are bound to see lots more interesting projects from Jordan in the future!

Like many of our inspiring young people, Jordan entered the BT Young Scientist Exhibition. In fact, he won first place in Junior Technology!

In 2020 Jordan helped Christmas tree farmers to sell their trees online via a website called Real Irish Trees.

Advice for Young Computer Programmers and Tech Entrepreneurs:
Start as soon as you can – you're never too young to start coding.

IZZY & AILBHE KEANE

DESIGNERS, ENTREPRENEURS, DISABILITY CAMPAIGNERS
1993 & 1997

When they were little, Galway sisters Ailbhe and Izzy Keane loved playing dress-up. As well as putting on fancy clothes and hats, they had great fun decorating Izzy's wheelchair.

And they still love decorating Izzy's wheels. In fact, they now run a business that transforms wheelchairs into fashion statements!

Izzy was born with spina bifida*. She is paralysed from her waist down and has used a wheelchair all her life. To Izzy, her wheelchair is a positive; it gives her freedom. She loves matching her wheels to her outfit. 'It's a great conversation opener too,' Izzy says.

Ailbhe dreamed up the idea for stylish, brightly coloured wheel covers in 2016. It was her final year project at NCAD (National College of Art and Design). It took a lot of hard work. 'I experimented and made loads of mistakes,' Ailbhe says. 'That's how I learned.'

When Ailbhe and Izzy posted photos and videos of Izzy and her wheel covers on Instagram, they went viral with millions of views. *Where can we get these wheels?* people asked.

So the sisters took a big leap of faith and set up their own company, Izzy Wheels. With Ailbhe as Creative Director and Izzy as Brand Ambassador, they have worked with over 100 top designers and produced thousands of wheel covers for children and adults all over the world.

As well as being great fun, they say running a business together has made them even closer!

Spina bifida is a medical condition that affects the spine. Some people with spina bifida can find it hard to walk.

There is a Barbie doll with Izzy Wheels on her wheelchair. Children can order matching Izzy Wheels for their own chair too.

Ailbhe and Izzy were the first Irish people to take over Instagram's official account. They reached 225 million people with their fun, colourful posts!

Advice for Young Entrepreneurs and Designers:
If you love art there are lots of opportunities and different jobs. Every business needs someone with a creative eye.

THE FUTURE'S SO BRIGHT!

COLLISON BROTHERS
BUSINESS & COMPUTING

Limerick brothers Patrick and John Collison set up the online global payments company, Stripe, in 2010. They have both loved computers since they were young; Patrick took his first computer course when he was eight. In 2016 they became the world's youngest self-made billionaires.

LAUREN McKEOWN
SPACE SCIENTIST

Lauren has always been passionate about space. In school – Loreto Beaufort, Dublin - she was voted 'most likely to work for NASA', the American space agency. In 2015 her dream came true when she became a NASA international intern. She now lectures at Birbeck University in London. Her subject? Space, of course!

JANE NÍ DHULCHAOINTIGH
INVENTOR

Jane grew up on a farm in Kilkenny where she was always fixing things. She became the first Irish person to win the European Inventor Award in 2018. Her invention? Sugru, a mouldable glue. It has now helped millions of people all over the world to fix things, from toys to headphones.

DR CONOR McGINN
ROBOTICS ENGINEER

Conor has been fascinated by robots since he was in school. He is now Assistant Professor (of Robotics) at Trinity College Dublin and CEO of Akara Robotics. With his team he created Stevie, a robot to help people at home, and Violet, a robot who cleans hospital rooms using UV light.

LOUISE EGAN
ENTREPRENEUR

Louise set up her I-Spy fitness clothing company with her mum when she was in Transition Year. Their aim was to design and create leggings and tops that were stylish, comfortable and perfect for working out in. Thousands of customers in Ireland and all over the world now wear their brand.

MAMOBO OGORO
DIGITAL MEDIA

Mamobo moved to Ireland from Nigeria when she was four. In 2020 she founded Gorm Media, a digital media company with diversity at its heart. Its mission is 'to unify communities by having young people use their voice'. Their video content features a wide range of young Irish people.

RÓISÍN NÍ RÍAIN

PARALYMPIC SWIMMER

2005

Aged sixteen, Róisín was the youngest athlete at the Tokyo 2020 Paralympics* (held in 2021 due to the pandemic) where she reached five swimming finals and swam four personal bests.

Róisín started swimming lessons at the age of four. At age nine she joined Limerick Swimming Club and has been with them ever since. She swam in her first competition in Nenagh, Co. Tipperary when she was ten and won gold in all five of her events. 'It was a great feeling,' she says. From then on, she was hooked on competitive swimming!

Being a competitive swimmer isn't easy. Róisín wakes up at 4.45am to swim for two hours before school, and swims for another two hours after school. She also does two or three gym sessions a week to keep herself strong. Luckily her family are very supportive, and she has the drive and the determination to keep going.

All her training has paid off. In 2020 she started competing in major world competitions, joining the World Para Swimming Series in Italy. She went on to win a bronze medal at the European Championship and represent Ireland at the Paralympics.

She doesn't always win her races. 'You're always going to have to deal with losing at some point. You need to accept what happened and move on quickly.'

Róisín is now training for the Paris 2024 Paralympics and hopes to reach the medal podium. With her dedication and talent, this Limerick teen is on her way!

The Paralympics are open to athletes with a range of disabilities. Róisín swims in the visually impaired disability group.

Róisín is an accomplished grade seven pianist. Her favourite musician is the Italian pianist Ludovico Einaudi who also composes music for movies. His latest album is called *Underwater*!

Both Róisin's parents are doctors, so it's no surprise that to unwind she loves watching medical dramas. A current favourite is *Grey's Anatomy*.

Róisín's Advice for Young Athletes:
Don't give up. There will always be setbacks, you need to be able to pick yourself up and bounce back from them. Keep going!

'I love setting little goals and trying to achieve them. It keeps me motivated.'

OISÍN O'CALLAGHAN

MOUNTAIN BIKER

2003

Limerick teenager Oisín O'Callaghan was named RTÉ Young Sportsperson of the Year in 2020 after winning the Downhill Mountain Bike Junior World Championships in Austria. He tore down the 2.3km course at speeds of almost 65km/h, taking the much-coveted winner's rainbow jersey. 'To make history in Ireland, to be the first downhill mountain bike world champion, was incredible,' he says.

Oisín has been mad about bikes since he was three, when he first rode a little bike without stabilisers in his garden. He remembers speeding down a grassy slope and into a flowerbed.

Bikes are in Oisín's blood. His dad, Chris, is a keen mountain biker and co-owner of Ballyhoura Trailriders bike and rental shop. Ballyhoura is Ireland's largest mountain bike trail network, in Ardpatrick. Chris also helps Oisín train.

Oisín started downhill-racing at age twelve. From the start he knew he wanted to be World Champion and in 2020 this dream came true in Austria when he took the title.

In 2021 he had a crash during the same championships and finished fifth. 'I scrambled to get back on the bike and I kept on fighting,' he says. He was disappointed, but put it behind him and focused on the next race.

Oisín is part of the YT Racing Dudes, a professional racing team. He trains hard every day, running, spending time in the gym, and training on his bike.

Oisín is now racing at the Elite (senior) level. His goal is to be one of the best riders in the world. With his talent and bravery, there is no doubt he will achieve his aim!

Oisín loves tractors. If he wasn't a bike racer he says, 'I'd probably be out in a field driving tractors.'

During lockdown Oisín built a cycling track with his friends. His nickname is 'Double O'.

Advice for Mountain Bikers: Have fun and don't get caught up trying to have the best results or social media.

'Ever since I was three or four
I wanted to be World Champion.'

'I try to focus on the next training session, the next game, just improving every day.'

GAVIN BAZUNU

In 2021 a nineteen-year-old Irish goalkeeper saved a penalty taken by one of the greatest footballers of all time, Cristiano Ronaldo. The goalkeeper's name was Gavin Bazunu.

He has been called one of the best young goalkeepers in Europe, and won RTÉ's Young Sportsperson of the Year Award in 2021. But where did it all start?

Gavin was born in Dublin and raised in Firhouse. He's always been mad about football. Gavin's mum, Cara, told RTÉ presenter Ray D'Arcy, 'He could never walk past a football. From the time he could walk there was always a football in front of him.'

When Gavin was around twelve he joined the FAI's Emerging Talent Programme. Coach and former League of Ireland goalkeeper Richie Fitzgibbon who worked with Gavin said he had 'serious potential' and 'standout skill', and 'even at that age it was – wow!'

In June 2018, aged sixteen, Gavin became the youngest ever player to play for Shamrock Rovers senior team. By the following February he had signed to Manchester City. He went on to play on loan at Rochdale and then Portsmouth.

After playing for the Republic of Ireland youth teams at under 17 and under 21 level, Gavin made his senior debut in 2021, a proud moment for him and all his family. In June 2022 he signed for Premier League team, Southampton.

As well as playing football, Gavin is also studying for an online degree in Sports Science.

Gavin is known for being cool, calm and mature, someone who thinks before he speaks. He takes all his success in his stride. 'I want to continue to build on all the things I've done,' he says.

Gavin loves listening to Irish musicians like Christy Moore and The Dubliners. He says, 'It makes you feel connected to home.'

Gavin's younger brother Todd is also a talented goalkeeper and they love playing FIFA together on Playstation.

Advice for Footballers:
Try to learn from your mistakes and move on quickly.
It's important to stay level-headed, but also to have passion and energy for each game.

RHASIDAT ADELEKE

ATHLETE
2002

In 2022 Tallaght athlete Rhasidat Adeleke broke record after record, becoming the fastest Irish woman ever at 60m, 200m, 300m and 400m and the fastest female teenager in Europe at the 300m. And she continues to topple records all the time! But how did she get started?

Dublin-born Rhasidat has always been mad about sport. She played basketball, Gaelic football and soccer in primary school and badminton, volleyball, Gaelic football and soccer in secondary school. 'I'm a very competitive person and I always give it my all,' she says.

At around age fourteen she decided to concentrate on athletics. 'I knew I was fast because I used to beat all the boys at sports day,' she says. On the advice of her PE teacher, she joined Tallaght Athletics Club and started training every day after school. Her mum, Ade, was a great support, driving her to training and competitions. 'She's been a huge influence,' Rhasidat says. 'I couldn't have done it all without her.'

At fifteen all the hard work paid off and Rhasidat won a gold medal at the European under-18s Championships. In 2021 she won the 100 metres and the 200 metres at the European Athletics Under-20s Championships, the 'sprint double'.

After finishing school, she won an athletics scholarship to the University of Texas where she can race against athletes from all over the world. She says, 'It's given me more confidence knowing that I've been competing against the world's best.'

One of Rhasidat's big goals is to motivate more Irish girls to take part in sport. 'There's so much talent here!' she says.

Rhasidat won the Under-20 Athlete of the Year at the Irish Life Health National Athletics Awards in 2021. She brought her mum, Ade, to the awards with her.

Rhasidat would like to represent Ireland in the 2024 Olympics. And we'd love to watch her run in Paris!

Advice for Young Athletes:
Find a local athletics club and join up.
Train as often as you can, and always give it your all.

'If you're in sport because you love it, it gives you a chance to become the athlete that you strive to be.'

'I truly believe if you are happy and with the people you love, you are winning in life.'

NHAT NGUYEN

BADMINTON PLAYER
2002

Nhat Nguyen moved to Ireland from Vietnam with his parents and sister when he was six. When he was nine, he started playing soccer for Woodlawn Football Club as a striker. But then his dad introduced him to badminton.

He turned out to be a natural and at age eleven started to beat his dad. 'Or maybe he let me win to build my confidence,' Nhat jokes.

A few years and a lot of hard work later, Nhat became the first Irish player to win the under-17 European badminton championships. In 2017 he won his first senior titles. He enjoys the challenge of playing older and more experienced players.

Nhat has won the Irish national badminton championships five times and qualified for the 2020 Tokyo Olympics (held in 2021), proudly representing his country. He lost in the opening game – to the tenth best player in the world.

'I used to dwell more on losing,' he says. 'But now I learn from it and move on. In badminton you're always winning and losing points.'

Nhat used to get up at 5.45am to train before school and train after school too. Now he's left school he trains full time, six days a week.

His short-term goal is to be one of the top thirty badminton players in the world (he's currently ranked 40th). He's also looking forward to the Olympics in Paris in 2024.

'We'll see what the future holds,' he says, 'but I'm feeling quite confident.'

Nhat comes from a sporty family; his sister Thammy is a weightlifter. She is also hoping to qualify for the Paris Olympics in 2024 – a brother and sister team!

Nhat has inspirational quotes stuck to the end of his bed where he can see them every day. They help to keep him inspired and focused.

Nhat's Advice for Young Badminton Players or Sports People:
Have fun and give it 100%.

KATIE McCABE

FOOTBALLER
1995

Number eleven. The number has special meaning for Katie McCabe. When she was little, she asked Santa for an Irish football jersey with number eleven on the back, the number of her favourite Irish footballer, Damien Duff. Now her own Irish jersey has the same number on the back and she's the youngest ever captain of the team.

'I'd never expected to be captain of Ireland at twenty-one,' she says. 'It's what I've always dreamed of.'

Katie worked hard to make that dream come true. She comes from a family of eleven children; from a young age she was outside kicking a ball around. She started off playing on boys' teams. 'I was kind of shy and nervous being the only girl,' she says. But she kept going. She played for both girls' and boys' teams until she turned thirteen.

At sixteen she signed with Raheny United and at twenty she moved to London after signing for Arsenal Ladies. Leaving Ireland wasn't easy, she missed all her friends and family, but once again, she kept going.

In December 2020 she made her 100th appearance for Arsenal Ladies. In April 2021 she earned her fiftieth cap for Ireland. In the same year she helped negotiate equal pay for the women's and men's national football teams. These were campaigns after her own heart, because Katie has always believed that everyone should be treated with equality and respect and is a proud supporter of LGBTQ+ rights.

Katie would like to win more trophies with Arsenal and to play for Ireland in a major tournament. One thing is sure, whatever Katie does in the future she'll give it her all!

Katie's jumper at Arsenal Ladies is number fifteen. She is described as a 'powerful, pacey winger who can also play full-back.'

Lauryn, Katie's sister, also plays football (Shamrock Rovers). Her brother, Gary played in the League of Ireland Premier Division for many years.

Advice for Young Footballers:
Working hard is number one. Don't miss training and keep your head down. Be confident in what you want to do. If you want to be a footballer don't let anything get in your way.

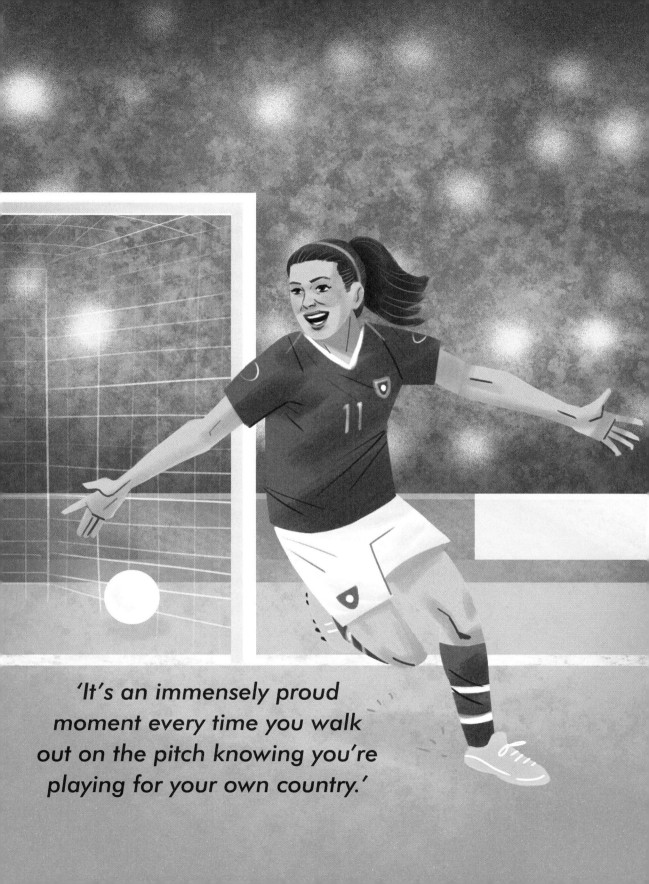

'It's an immensely proud moment every time you walk out on the pitch knowing you're playing for your own country.'

KEEP IT UP!

KELLIE HARRINGTON
Boxer

Kellie started boxing at St Mary's Boxing Club when she was fifteen. They turned her away as they didn't take girls, but she persisted. and went on to win gold at the Tokyo 2020 Olympics. She was joint Grand Marshal at the St Patrick's Day Parade in her beloved Dublin city in 2022.

AYEISHA McFERRAN
Hockey Player

Ayeisha started playing hockey at age seven and played her first match for the Irish senior team on her eighteenth birthday. She was named Goalkeeper of the Tournament at the 2018 Women's Hockey World Cup final.

ZAK MORADI
Hurler

Zak was born in Iraq and was eleven when his country was invaded. Zak and his family had to flee, moving to Carrick-on-Shannon, Co. Leitrim. He started playing hurling, joining the Leitrim team in 2010. He is the first Iraqi-born hurler to win a GAA medal.

RACHAEL BLACKMORE
JOCKEY

Rachael learned to ride when she was very young. She won her first pony race when she was thirteen. In 2021 she became the first female jockey to win the Grand National. That year she was named RTÉ Sportsperson of the Year and BBC World Sport Star of the Year.

RHYS McCLENAGHAN
GYMNAST

Rhys is from Newtownards, Co. Down and hopes to be the first Irish Olympic medallist in his sport, gymnastics. He won a bronze medal at the 2019 World Championships on the pommel horse and competed at the Toyko 2020 Olympics, coming seventh place overall.

PAUL O'DONOVAN
ROWER

Paul started rowing at Skibbereen Rowing Club when he was around seven and has been winning medals in his sport since he was young. In 2016 he won an Olympic silver medal with his brother, Gary, and in 2020 he won a gold Olympic medal with Fintan McCarthy.

'Follow your heart. Even if it's hard, it will make you happy.' Amelia O'Mahony Brady

'Stand out from the crowd – be authentically you, always.' James McCann

JAMES McCANN &
AMELIA O'MAHONY BRADY

FASHION DESIGNER & FASHION WRITER
2007 & 1998

James can't remember a time when he wasn't hooked on fashion. He got a sewing machine for his eighth birthday and signed up for a Project Fashion course. In 2019 he won Project Fashion Young Designer of the Year. He's made clothes from all kinds of things, from car seat material to IKEA bags. For James, fashion is all about being different and expressing yourself. He hopes to study fashion in London or New York. His goal is to design clothes that aren't aimed at boys or girls, but can be worn by anyone. With his passion and determination, we are bound to be wearing James McCann designs one day.

Amelia O' Mahony Brady lives and breathes fashion. As a little girl, she collected fashion magazines and studied styles and trends.

Her mum was a fashion designer and always encouraged Amelia to wear the clothes she wanted to wear. 'I experienced bullying at school for being different,' Amelia says. 'But I kept on being myself.'

At thirteen Amelia set up her own fashion blog, La Femme Éclectique, and by seventeen she was working for *Le Cool Dublin* magazine as an intern, writing about … you guessed it, fashion! She now writes about fashion for a variety of Irish and Italian magazines, reports on it for RTÉ Radio and was the fashion editor of *Totally Dublin*. Her dream is to work as a fashion and art curator and to manage fashion archives.

James' Advice for Young Fashion Designers:
Don't let anyone tell you your clothes are too out of the box. Follow your own artistic vision.

Amelia's Advice for Young Fashion Fans:
Research fashion in a way that feels fun. You could even create a physical scrapbook!

Remember there are so many roles in the fashion industry beyond being a designer – you could be a trend forecaster, a stylist or even a fashion professor! Stay true to what you love and you'll always find the right path.

EVA MCPARLAND

ARTIST

2006

Eva won her first art competition at the age of eleven, a still life in oil pastels. Since then, she has won many other art competitions including the prestigious Zurich Young Portrait Prize in 2020, with a coloured pencil portrait of her sister, Ellen, who was ten at the time.

Eva drew Ellen wearing a mask as she wanted to highlight what children had been going through during the Covid-19 pandemic. It was featured on the front page of several newspapers.

Eva says, 'I love creating art that reflects current events. I hope that through my art I can compel viewers to see those events from a different perspective.'

She hasn't always been successful when entering art competitions. 'It's important to see the losses as an opportunity to learn,' she says. 'You can't take it too seriously, not let it get you down and keep on going.'

She gets inspiration from the world around her, and its energy and movement. 'I try to capture the sense of a person or place,' she says. 'Art is a way of recording life and reflecting it.'

After school, Eva is interested in studying a subject like science, maths or history at college but says, 'Art will always be an important part of my life.'

For now, she will continue creating beautiful, meaningful artwork, one drawing or painting at a time.

Eva plays Gaelic sports and loves sea swimming in the summer. 'When I'm swimming, I'm really in the present,' she says 'like when I'm making art.'

Eva loves the work of Jack B. Yeats. 'I find him really inspiring,' she says. 'He never tried to explain his paintings; he let people decide what they meant for themselves. There's a lot of feeling and emotion in his paintings.'

Eva's Tips for Young Artists:
Enter art competitions but don't let failure get you down, keep going!
Be true to yourself and try not to copy other people's work. Draw what you enjoy and try to draw from life if you can.

'When you think like an artist, you're always looking for inspiration; you notice things other people might not notice.'

'I live and breathe music.'

MICHAEL MOLONEY

SINGER/SONGWRITER
2006

Michael Moloney played his first gig when he was nine, in his dad's music pub in Ballina.

Michael comes from a very musical family; his grandmother on his dad's side taught piano and his grandfather on his mum's side played melodeon. Two of his uncles are musicians.

In 2020 Michael played to the biggest crowd of his life to date – millions of television viewers – when he appeared on *The Late Late Toy Show*. He sang 'Giants' by Irish singer-songwriter, Dermot Kennedy – and showed enormous poise as Dermot appeared beside him, singing along.

'I got such a shock,' Michael says, 'but I told myself to just keep going. I was having so much fun singing, I didn't want it to end.'

The show gave him huge exposure and lots of new fans on social media, but he never let it go to his head, he focused on his music and kept playing, appearing at gigs all over the country and a music festival in Bundoran.

In 2021 he released his first single – 'All That I Do' – which reached number one in the Irish ITunes chart. It's a very special song as he wrote it about his dad, Emmett, who died in 2017 when Michael was ten. His dad was a huge music fan and a big supporter of Michael's own music.

The single was recorded in Windmill Lane, where acts like U2 and Kate Bush have also recorded. 'The whole experience was super cool,' he says.

He is signed to Universal Music Ireland and hopes to release an album of his own songs one day. 'I love music,' he says. 'I never want to stop playing.'

Michael plays six instruments: guitar, piano, drums, ukulele, tin whistle and violin. He has three different music teachers to keep him on his toes!

Dermot Kennedy started playing the guitar when he was ten. He is now one of Ireland's best loved singer-songwriters. He gave Michael a Fender left-handed guitar, as, like Michael, Dermot is left-handed.

Michael's Advice for Young Musicians:
If you learn just three chords on the guitar you can play all kinds of songs.

SARAH FITZGERALD

BOOK CHAMPION, RESEARCHER, WRITER
2004

Sarah Fitzgerald from Co. Cork has loved books all her life. Her earliest memory is of pestering her parents to read her bedtime stories. She wanted to share this love with children and young people, so in 2017 she set up Sarah's Book Project – a website full of great reviews and book news – and she's been championing and promoting books ever since.

By second year of senior school, Sarah noticed that most people in her class were not reading for fun. In 2018 she entered the BT Young Scientist Exhibition with a project based on her research about the decline of reading in Irish children. She continued her research, with her friend Anna Peare, for a project in 2020. They proved that reading improves your ability to problem solve.

Sarah was chosen to be a judge for the national KPMG Children's Books Ireland Books of the Year Awards, reading almost a hundred books, and has also been an Ambassador for Cruinniú na nÓg, the national day of creativity for children and young people.

In 2020 she was awarded a Garda National Youth Award for her Book Cloud project, which encourages communities to gather unwanted books and give them to people who'd like to read them.

As well as researching and reading, Sarah loves writing and has won awards for her short stories and poems. She has been published by *Assembly* magazine, run by the Malala Fund, and she interviewed Marley Dias, founder of the 1,000 Black Girl Books project for *Inis* magazine.

In the future she'd like to study English in college and work as a journalist, editor, or maybe a writer. For now, she's busy researching, writing and doing her very favourite thing – reading!

Sarah once appeared on *The Late Late Toy Show* – reviewing books of course! Her favourite book of all time is *Little Women* by Louisa May Alcott. Other favourites are books by Jacqueline Wilson and Judi Curtin.

Sarah is also passionate about the environment and won first prize in the senior category at the Young Reporters for the Environment Ireland Awards for her project titled 'How climate-smart are our smartphones?'

Sarah's Tips for Making a Difference:
Find something that you're passionate about. If you're passionate about the issue you'll want to keep fighting.

'Nature is as big a part of me as my own heartbeat.'

DARA McANULTY

Dara McAnulty lives with his family and rescue greyhound, Rosie, at the foot of the Mourne Mountains in Co. Down. He has loved the natural world since he was small. He says, 'I crawled to catch anything that moved … Every screech, squawk, flicker of wings, wriggle, buzz filled me with a desire to learn more and more.'

In June 2016 he started to write a nature blog, writing about all kinds of animals and plants that interested him, from bats to butterflies. It started to get a lot of attention and to win awards.

In 2017 Dara won a BBC Springwatch Unsprung Wildlife Hero Award and started to appear on radio, television and at live events talking about his beloved nature. Although he finds public speaking stressful, he pushes himself to do it to share his passion for wildlife and the environment.

When he was fourteen, he published his first book, *Diary of a Young Naturalist*. It tells the story of a year in Dara's life. He writes about his deep relationship with nature and the joys and challenges of being autistic. 'Being autistic allows me to think about things in a different way, to see things from a different angle,' he says.

Dara's book was hugely successful, winning many awards including the Wainwright Prize for Nature Writing. Dara became the youngest writer in the world to win a major literary award.

He currently writes a nature column for the *Irish Times* and recently published his first book for children, *Wild Child*. He is one of the world's most gifted nature writers and we can't wait to read what he writes next!

Dara loves the Percy Jackson books. His favourite is *Percy Jackson and the Battle of the Labyrinth*. He says, 'Dedalus is a great character and this book taught me valuable lessons about the difference between knowledge and wisdom.'

Dara is mad about mushrooms. His favourite is the Devil's Fingers or Octopus Stinkhorn, 'because they are simultaneously gross and exceptionally cool. Like a scarlet claw, motionless on the grass!'

Advice for Young Writers:
Write from your heart, your knowledge and your imagination. Writing is truly personal and should be unique to your true style. Don't imitate, we need every kind of voice and vision.

AMYBETH MCNULTY

ACTOR

2001

Imagine getting the chance to star in the screen adaptation of a book you love. That's what happened to Irish teenager Amybeth McNulty!

Amybeth was fourteen when she was chosen to play Anne in the hugely popular Netflix series *Anne with an E*, beating around 1,800 other young actors from around the world. The series is based on the much-loved *Anne of Green Gables* books by Lucy Maud Montgomery, which depict life on Prince Edward Island in Canada in the 1800s.

Although her mum was born in Canada, Amybeth grew up in Letterkenny, Co. Donegal. She loved playing Anne and feels they have similar personalities. She says, 'Anne has so much love for the world, which I think I share with her.' She also relates to Anne's 'curiosity about everything, and how she can be so fierce and so bold but so gentle and so loving.'

As a child, Amybeth studied ballet and theatre at An Grianán Theatre in Letterkenny. She spent so much time there that 'people used to joke I probably had a sleeping bag under the stage.'

When she was ten, Amybeth played Marta von Trapp in *The Sound of Music* in London. Her first screen role was in the RTÉ series *Clean Break*, and she hasn't stopped working since. In season four of the Netflix series *Stranger Things*, she plays Vickie, a 'cool, fast-talking band nerd'.

As well as acting, Amybeth is 'intrigued by the camera' and might consider film school in the future. For now, she's setting our screens alight as one of the most exciting and vibrant young actors ever to have come out of Ireland.

Amybeth describes herself as a 'bookworm'. She read the *Anne of Green Gables* books when she was nine.

Like Anne, Amybeth loved using her imagination as a child. She was home schooled and used to have adventures in the forest with her friends. They created a world together called the Land of Dreams.

Advice for Young Actors: There are lots of youth theatre groups around the country like An Grianán Youth Theatre where Amybeth started her acting career. You can find a list of them on the Youth Theatre Ireland website (youththeatre.ie).

ZAINAB BOLADALE

JOURNALIST & WRITER

1996

Zainab was born in Lagos, Nigeria and moved to Ennis, Co. Clare with her mum, younger brother and sister when she was four. She has always loved talking to people and hearing their stories, so she decided to become a journalist. She went to Dublin City University to study journalism and was named Journalist of the Year at the university's Hybrid Awards in 2017. Zainab was so good at telling other people's stories that she was snapped up by RTÉ's *News2Day* as a presenter. 'It was super exciting,' she says. 'I almost didn't believe it!'

For *News2Day*, she interviewed children in schools up and down the country. 'Children are more tuned in than adults realise. They have a lot to say about the world.' Maybe Zainab has visited your school!

As the first Nigerian-Irish news presenter on RTÉ, and one of the youngest, at only twenty, she is also a trailblazer. 'I didn't grow up in an Ireland where I saw someone that looked like me on the screen, but that has changed.'

In 2019 she moved to *Nationwide*, an RTÉ show that presents news from around the country. While working there she has experienced racism*and has some advice on this: 'It's important to let people know what has happened so it can be stopped early on. Tell someone.'

Zainab has lots of exciting plans for the future. She would like to make documentaries for young audiences and to study screenwriting. Watch this space – with Zainab's talent, focus and energy, she's destined for great things.

Racism is when people are treated unfairly or bullied because of their skin colour or background. It takes many different forms and can cause great harm.

Zainab hopes to follow in the footsteps of her favourite authors Malorie Blackman and Jacqueline Wilson and write her own book for teenagers one day.

Zainab is a co-founder of Beyond Representation, an organisation that champions women of colour in the Irish media, business and the arts.

Zainab's Tips for Young Journalists:
Start with the tools you already have no matter how big or small. Create YouTube videos, make podcasts or write articles for your school newspaper or website.

'Journalism is about telling real stories. Follow things that are interesting to you.'

THEIR NAMES IN LIGHTS

EVANNA LYNCH

Actor & Writer

Evanna Lynch became internationally famous at fourteen, making her film debut in *Harry Potter and the Order of the Phoenix*. She auditioned at an open casting call in London against 15,000 other girls. She now combines acting with writing and published her first book (a memoir) in 2021.

RYAN TUBRIDY

TELEVISION PRESENTER & WRITER

Ryan Tubridy started reviewing movies and books on RTÉ radio and television shows aged twelve. Now he's one of Ireland's most popular broadcasters, best known to children as the host of *The Late Late Toy Show*. He has also written several bestselling books for both children and adults.

SAOIRSE RONAN

ACTOR

Saoirse Ronan first appeared on television in Irish medical drama *The Clinic* aged nine. She received her first Academy Award nomination at thirteen for her role in *Atonement*. She has become one of the world's most acclaimed actors and won a Golden Globe Award in 2018 for her performance as a teenager in *Lady Bird*.

PAUL MESCAL
ACTOR

Paul Mescal first performed on stage when he was sixteen, playing the Phantom in his school's production of *The Phantom of the Opera*. Since then, he has starred in many plays, films and television shows and has won many awards for his acting.

DENISE CHAILA
MUSICIAN & RAPPER

Denise Chaila moved to Ireland from Zambia with her family when she was young. She started performing in Limerick as a teenager and describes herself as a 'pocket-sized dreamer with a planet-sized voice'. She won the Choice Music Award in 2021 for her album, *Go Bravely*, and a Music Moves Europe Award in 2022.

GEARÓID SOLAN
BALLET DANCER

At fifteen Gearóid started studying at the Royal Ballet Upper School in London, the first Irish male dancer to be accepted to the school in thirty years. He joined Boston Ballet in 2020 and has danced in many famous ballets such as *Giselle* and *The Nutcracker*.

'Be kind to people, have fun, and always remember to hug the ones you love the most.'

ADAM KING

KINDNESS CAMPAIGNER

2014

In 2020 six-year-old Adam King appeared on *The Late Late Toy Show*. On the show he gave a 'virtual hug' to John Doyle, his porter friend at Temple Street Children's Hospital. The hug is a piece of artwork that Adam originally created for his teacher as he missed her during the first Covid lockdown.

After the show, messages started to flood in for Adam from all over the world, including from astronaut Chris Hadfield, and NASA, the American space agency.

Adam is a regular visitor to hospital as he has a brittle bone condition called OI (Osteogenesis Imperfecta), which means his bones break easily. He is a wheelchair user and can also take some steps. He is the second youngest in his family and has four brothers and sisters, Danny, Robert, Katie and Sarah.

With the help of his family and friends Adam's hug went national and then global, capturing the hearts of people all over the world. The hug became a symbol of connection during the difficult Covid times. His hug was flown in space by Virgin Galactic on a test flight! Adam has helped raise over €250,000 for Irish hospitals through his hug.

He even got a letter from the US President, Joe Biden. Adam says, 'He wrote about the hug and he told me never to give up.' The letter was hand delivered by the Taoiseach, Micheál Martin.

One day Adam might like to be a NASA Capsule Communicator or CapCom, the person on the ground who helps the astronauts in space, a writer, a television presenter, or a paralympic athlete. The sky's the limit!

Adam has a very special toy rabbit called Bubby. Adam has lots of friends who he loves playing with, but Bubby is one of his best.

As well as art, Adam loves playing soccer with Youghal United Football For All, reading, visiting his local library, and board games. He also loves dance and performs with the Sinéad Sheppard School of Performing Arts.

Adam has inspired an animated show called *Adam ♥ Adventure*! It's the first Irish children's programme to have a wheelchair user as the hero.

FLOSSIE DONNELLY

CLIMATE CHANGE & MARINE ACTIVIST

2007

Every week people who love the sea head out to Irish beaches to pick up plastic and rubbish, thanks to Flossie and the Beach Cleaners. The charity and action group was set up by Flossie Donnelly when she was nine.

It all started when Flossie and her family visited Thailand; she was upset by all the rubbish in the sea and wanted to do something to help so she decided to set up a beach cleaning group at home.

Flossie put posters up, but not one person turned up at the very first beach clean. 'It was just me and my mum and dad,' Flossie says. But that didn't put her off. She kept going and now Flossie and the Beach Cleaners has teams all over the country.

The beach cleaners fill special cloth sacks with the rubbish and weigh them. Their record for one day's clean to date is a whopping 545kg or almost 5 ½ tonnes of rubbish, taken from beaches in every county in Ireland.

Flossie believes that every beach clean matters. 'Every 1kg you take off the beach is less rubbish in a sea animal's stomach,' she explains.

She is hoping that her organisation will inspire future environmentalists; they plan to send Transition Year students to Indonesia to help clean the Citarum River or 'plastic river' and learn about what plastics, pollution and climate change are doing to communities in other countries.

One day Flossie would like to study Marine Biology and use her knowledge to work with sharks and jellyfish. Until then she's looking after Ireland's beaches and seas, one beach clean at a time!

Every Friday you can see Flossie outside the Dáil, the Irish Government Buildings, where she has been climate striking since December 2018.

Flossie's love for the planet, but most especially the oceans and seas, comes from her mother, Harriet, who is passionate about the sea. 'My mum would do anything to go swimming with marine animals,' Flossie says.

Advice for Young Activists: Pick one thing you care about to help with climate change and actively work to help solve it.

'No one is too young to make a difference.'

SAOI O'CONNOR

CLIMATE ACTIVIST
2002

Saoi O'Connor's activism started early. When Saoi was four, they dressed in a banana costume to promote fair trade in the Skibbereen St Patrick's Day parade.

On Friday 11 January 2019, at age sixteen, Saoi started climate striking outside Cork City Hall. Saoi says, 'I saw climate strikes happening in other parts of the world and I thought, right, that's awesome. We could do that. There wasn't one happening near me, so I just started one.'

It was the first chapter of a journey that has taken Saoi all over the world, campaigning for global climate justice with the Fridays for Future movement. Saoi travelled to the European Parliament in Strasbourg in 2019 to take part in climate debates and was one of the delegates at the RTÉ Youth Assembly on Climate in the same year. Saoi lobbied politicians at the COP26* in Glasgow in 2021.

Fridays for Future aims to keep global temperature rise below 1.5 degrees Celsius. To do this, Ireland must be at net zero carbon emissions by 2030. Saoi says, 'Climate change is an issue that affects us all globally and you can observe its effects here in Ireland in so many ways. We now have more extreme weather and more frequent storms.'

Saoi will keep fighting for climate justice until the Irish and world governments and politicians listen. 'We don't have time to wait,' Saoi says. 'We must act now or we may not have a future.'

*COP is a United Nations Conference of the Parties where all countries meet to talk about climate change. In 2021 the 26th annual summit took place in Glasgow, Scotland.

Saoi is also a writer. They contributed a piece called 'Untitled' to an anthology called *Empty House* which asked writers to respond to the climate crisis.

In 2021 Saoi was awarded the Young Humanitarian of the Year at the Irish Red Cross Humanitarian Awards for their 'inspiring leadership as a climate activist'.

Saoi's Advice for Activists:
Climate strikes show that everyone can have a voice and can effect change.
Find other activists in your school or community and join together to make some noise!

'The climate crisis is not a crisis of emissions, it's a crisis of injustice, it cannot be solved with science alone, it must also be healed by the people.'

'I try to bring change.'

IAN McDONAGH

EDUCATION & COMMUNITY ACTIVIST
2001

When Ian McDonagh was seventeen, he presented a paper to the government of Ireland. He said, 'It is my honour to be here today to speak about my views of the education system as a young Traveller.' He went on to explain that only 13 per cent of Traveller children complete secondary school.

Ian has been campaigning to make things better for people all his life. He was Chair of the Student Council in his school for five years, he has organised many clean-ups and fought to get speed ramps and play facilities put into his local area in Galway city. Above all, he is determined to encourage more Traveller children to stay in school. He says 'If you have a good education you can speak up for yourself and communicate with a much wider range of people. It's a weapon for life.'

Traveller history and culture is now on the school curriculum and Ian hopes there will be more Traveller role models in school books in the future. He feels it's a way of educating people about Traveller culture and dealing with racism* against Travellers.

During the pandemic Ian worked as a Senior Healthcare Assistant in Bushfield Nursing Home as well as studying for his Leaving Certificate. He's also an embalmer in a funeral home and is training to be a funeral director at The Irish College of Funeral Directing & Embalming. This might sound like an unusual choice, but he'd love to run his own funeral home one day. With his drive and determination, watch this space!

Racism is when people are treated unfairly or bullied because of their skin colour or background. It can take many different forms; for Travellers it is something they live with every day.

Ian was the first Traveller to enter the BT Young Scientist Exhibition. He's entered twice – both projects won awards. His projects looked at the role of the moon in the birth of foals, and cures and folklore in the Irish Traveller Community.

Ian presented his report on Traveller cures to Charles, Prince of Wales and Camilla, Duchess of Cornwall at an event at the President's House, Áras an Uachtaráin, in 2017.

Ian's Advice for Community Activists:
Always be yourself, follow your dreams and be proud of your community. Never let anyone else's opinions bring you down.

ELEANOR WALSH

ACTOR & AUTISM ACTIVIST
1995

When Eleanor was eight, she saw her first play called *The Bus*. 'From that day on I wanted to be on the stage,' she says.

Her hard work and determination have paid off and she has now appeared in critically acclaimed plays, including *What I (Don't) Know About Autis*m on the Peacock Stage at the Abbey Theatre. It's a play that celebrates autistic* identity and educates neurotypical* audiences.

Eleanor was diagnosed as autistic when she was around five. At secondary school she found it hard to make and keep friends. She recalls, 'I thought I was bad at life.'

When she joined Kilkenny Youth Theatre at eleven it changed her life. She appeared in many plays and also worked behind the scenes as an assistant director. 'It showed me that working in theatre was something that someone from Kilkenny could actually do as a career,' she says. 'I also made some great friends.'

As well as being an actor, Eleanor is a storyteller and singer. She also works as an autism advocate and is a Youth Ambassador for AsIAm, Ireland's National Autism Charity.

She hopes there will be many more parts for autistic actors in the future and is currently writing her first play. Whatever she does, Eleanor knows theatre will always be her passion. 'Theatre shows us ourselves and each other,' she says. 'It's unique.'

Autism is a neurological (brain) difference that affects how people experience the world and how they communicate with others. Every autistic person is different and has different experiences and challenges.

Neurotypical people are not autistic or diagnosed with other neurodivergent conditions (e.g. dyslexia, ADHD, dyspraxia).

For her first acting job, Eleanor dressed up as a medieval woman and told stories on the streets of Kilkenny. She loves Irish mythology and her favourite story to tell is 'How the Gaels Came to Ireland'.

In 2020 Eleanor appeared in *These Four Walls*, a short play by Sinéad Burke. It was watched online by thousands of people all over the world.

Eleanor's Advice for Young Actors
See and read plays. Find and join your local youth theatre through Youth Theatre Ireland. Write and put on your own plays with your friends. Make films and have fun!

MAKING A DIFFERENCE

ADAM HARRIS
SOCIAL ENTREPRENEUR
Adam is the Founder and CEO of AsIAm, an organisation working to build an Ireland where every autistic person can 'live and succeed as they are'.

Adam was diagnosed with Asperger's Syndrome when he was young. His own experiences inspired him to set up AsIAm while still studying for his Leaving Certificate.

SINÉAD BURKE
DISABILITY ACTIVIST & WRITER
Standing three feet, five inches tall, Dubliner Sinéad Burke dreams of a world where every person is encouraged and celebrated equally. She is the founder and CEO of Tilting the Lens, a consultancy that helps make sure things like fashion are accessible for everyone.

JOANNE O'RIORDAN
JOURNALIST & DISABILITY CAMPAIGNER
Joanne is a sports journalist for the *Irish Times*, with a particular interest in women's sport. One of only seven people in the world with Total Amelia, which means she has no limbs, Joanne has never let it stop her. She has given TEDx talks and a speech at the United Nations.

EILEEN FLYNN
Traveller activist & Senator

Eileen became a senator in 2020 after being nominated by the Taoiseach. She is the first Traveller to serve in the Oireachtas, or the national parliament. 'It's important to bring a Traveller voice to the table,' she says. She has been a Traveller activist for over ten years and wants to make sure all citizens of Ireland are treated equally and have equal opportunities.

HAZEL CHU
Politician & Former Lord Mayor of Dublin

In 2019 Hazel became the first Chinese-Irish person to be elected as a county councillor. She topped the poll! She became the Lord Mayor of Dublin in 2020, the first person of colour to hold the role. In fact, she was the first person of Chinese heritage to be mayor of any capital city in Europe – a true trailblazer!

There are many different roles in a publishing company and lots of people involved in bringing a book to life – but all of them love books! Michael O'Brien founded The O'Brien Press with his father Thomas in 1974 and since then it has established a reputation for excellence in publishing. Ivan O'Brien is the Managing Director and Kunak McGann the Rights Director. Editorial Administrator Megan Doolan and Accounts Manager Sinéad Lalor hold the fort in the office. Editors Helen Carr, Susan Houlden, Eoin O'Brien and Nicola Reddy work alongside Design Manager Emma Byrne and Production Manager Bex Sheridan to make the books. Then the Sales, Publicity and Marketing team – Brenda Boyne, Elena Browne, Chloe Coome, Laura Feeney, Aoife Harrison and Ruth Heneghan tell the world about them and get them out to readers and onto bookshop shelves.

First published 2022 by
The O'Brien Press Ltd.
12 Terenure Road East,
Rathgar, Dublin 6, D06 HD27, Ireland.
Tel: +353 1 4923333; Fax: +353 1 4922777
E-mail: books@obrien.ie; Website: obrien.ie
The O'Brien Press is a member of Publishing Ireland.

ISBN: 978-1-78849-328-4

10 9 8 7 6 5 4 3 2 1
26 25 24 23 22

Printed by L&C Printing Group, Poland.
The paper in this book is produced using pulp from managed forests.

Be Inspired! Young Irish People Changing the World
receives financial assistance from the Arts Council

Published in:
DUBLIN
UNESCO
City of Literature